To Nolan

ONWARD

Words to Encourage and Inspire

By Marlon P. Weaver

Photography by Amanda Lee Jennings

Thank you for your Service

Marlon Weaver

11 Jun 13

ISBN: 1460904230
ISBN-13: 978-1460904237

ONWARD
By Marlon P. Weaver

Introduction

Some of life's most inspiring quotes originate from some of the seemingly simplest observations. Just a slight change of perspective in any situation can mean the difference between discouragement and encouragement.

It has been said that a picture is worth a thousand words. It is my perspective that a word can be worth a thousand pictures.

The quotations in this book are timeless and reflect the wisdom and inspiration that can be acquired through everyday situations. Some of these thoughts can be profound enough to change lives or simple enough to just enjoy the moment.

These quotes were originally conceived as a memoir for my then infant daughter while I was in military service overseas. Giving her the treasure of wisdom would be the best way to share that experience with her and accompany her onward through life's journey.

Allow the words, thoughts and reflections in this book to be your companion through moments of tears and trouble onward to triumph. Use these words to produce laughter, excitement and understanding, by reading a quote per day or all at once.

Please accept this book as an invitation to a good conversation, and be inspired to move onward for the moment or for a lifetime.

Dedications

This is a special dedication to James Kingsbury, whose indomitable spirit is an inspiration to many. His strength in times of adversity is a reflection of the love he gives to his family and friends. We reciprocate that example as we show love one to another.

This is a special dedication to the men and women who serve our country at every level, even to place themselves in harm's way to keep us safe. Your sacrifice and commitment is greatly appreciated and never forgotten.

This is a special dedication to they who watch over us as parents, leaders, and educators. Thank you for setting the example, and showing that words and actions should complement each other. You continue to show us the right way and are there for us when the way is not so clear.

Say "I love you" to your children.

It does get better, especially when we are there for them when it doesn't.

The reason I **smile** is because
it is an outward expression of
something inside of me that refuses
to be defeated or destroyed by
anything that comes against it.
I **smile** because it is an invitation
to a small part of something great
enough to make a difference.

When it's raining instead of worrying that the sun isn't shining, consider how much the rain is helping to wash away.

Marlon P. Weaver

He will make a way even to the point of
becoming the way.

The opportunity to show **love** presents itself in different ways and the only way to present **love** is with our whole heart.

Cherish yesterday, embrace today,
love tomorrow and dream in between.

No matter what I've seen or what I've done, whether I had more pain than I've had fun, the expression on my face is only a small part of what I feel inside. I am **in** love.

Make a **plan**, work the **plan** then make the **plan** better so it will work. Finally, do not let pride stop you from asking for help.

It never matters without the element of common sense.

Although the love from someone's heart is strong enough to stand on, do not treat it like pavement and walk all over it.

Give the **happiness** that you want to receive, be the **good** that you would like to experience and return the **joy** that was placed in your life.

Life has a rhythm, if you're not going to dance to it then at least nod your head.

How you view my person or my actions is not important to me. What is important is giving my daughter a good life.

Sometimes the little steps can leave the biggest footprints.

An open ear goes well with a closed mouth.

We're not truly rich until we've understood the life of the poor.

Sometimes things do make sense.

You aren't hungry enough because you keep eating whatever people put on your plate. Slow down chew the food; masticate.

Don't do what you do instead master it. Never "coulda woulda" instead go after it. Look at your reflection instead of passing it. When you see a shadow do not go back to it.

Marlon P. Weaver

You can't beat the clock because it's two hands can hit harder.

22

There are no winners or losers at the finish line only professional starters.

Words don't break my bones; I don't let them get that close.

It's hard to do anything for anyone who isn't doing something for themselves.

Marlon P. Weaver

100 will agree with you, 10 will offer to help but there is always 1 that shows up.

26

Positively posture for progressive procurement.

We have power; it's a good
day to be happy.

Be yourself; go succeed where others have tried and failed.

Finding the right person should start
with the mirror.

Make the right moment instead of waiting for one.

Marlon P. Weaver

"No" is one word away from the greatest advice ever received.

There is no step too small to
leave an impression.

Let's observe Mother's Day but let us, to the more, celebrate our children who are the reason the day exists at all.

A tree without roots is really just a log, but can be used for so many different things.

The next time we do something nice make sure it's selfless with no strings attached.

People that hate on you the most
understand you the least; but love them
not because you have to but because
they need you to.

Trust is a luxury that I can't afford but I will go broke because I love you.

Today is ours. Let's enjoy it and I encourage you to do something for at least one other person.

Keep it real otherwise anything
else we do is a lie...

Moonlight is the sun's way of
saying, "I'm still with you."

God could have sent angels to watch over, provide for and protect us, but He sent MOM so that it would be done perfectly and with Love.

Onward

Please pass me by so I could have room
for good people.

It's time to put some tulips in this house.

Is there someone who you would like to thank and why?

How are you doing at this moment?

It's one thing if a dog steals your food, but if you give the food away to the dog don't complain about being hungry.

One thing at time, it's the wisest way
I can take. With thankfulness, it's the
best way I can make.

Institutions, if you are going to increase patronage and increase prices then it would be wise to increase the amount of available parking.

To some degree, we place much emphasis upon subjects that don't matter and not enough is applied to subjects that do matter. What matters to you?

Let the steps I take and the decisions
I make carry me forward and beyond
my last mistake.

Marlon P. Weaver

Enjoy this day, be productive
and have fun.

52

Love doesn't hurt; loving does, and sometimes it's worth the pain.

It's never easy. But realize that our every decision, good or bad, has value. Regrets are just the minor cost of embracing the priceless opportunity to change when and what we need to.

I would rather be wrong when I write
than to be right when I do wrong.

Life happens between each breath,
make those breaths count.

What is your thought for the day?

You are unique. There is something that only you can do. Be that, in love, for someone who matters to you and even more to they who need to know they matter to you.

The invisible can make the visible indivisible.

Sometimes I don't want to face the music, but I definitely don't want to turn my back to it.

Even as we take God for granted He does not treat us as our sins deserve.

Think about this. When somebody is asking for advice they may really just want to know if you still love them if they make the wrong decision.

Ignorance is like a canker sore in the mouth of society.

What it really means is we are all just trying to get some food.

Don't just settle for breaking
ground but try bringing in the dirt!!!

You know you are doing well when people have something to complain about.

Let's observe Father's Day but let us, to the more, celebrate our children who are the reason the day exists at all.

Thank you for showing the way,
providing the way, becoming the way...
Help me to do this for someone else...

Sometimes I want to be like a prism;
get placed in the light and then
spread wisdom...

I enjoy a good complaint once in a
while, but great solutions
are more my style...

What stresses you out today?

The best thing about today is that we learned from the worst of yesterday to give the hope of a greater tomorrow.

Someone has positively affected your life, just take a moment to tell them thank you... (Thank you)

Trust me, I don't have time to stress about what you think or don't think about me. If you want to feel better about yourself, eat some mac n cheese, it's "comfort" food.

We have come so far and yet we have gone so far. Can we stand still for just a second and let things come so we can get to where we need to go.

What have you accomplished so far today?

Onward

Use the alphabet as an unlimited
resource to writing something
good to someone.

Time to chill just a little

Be blessed; allow Him to make a way for you. Allow yourself to be a blessing for someone else...

What's important to you today?

One thing I am thankful for is the ability to be thankful for so many things.

College: one can major in debt and
minor in education.

Onward

I can only be me and right now that
means being productive

Fall in love with driving, it's like
watching a silent film; popcorn?

Making a difference is good and being the difference is great.

Marlon P. Weaver

Faith without works is dead, but work without faith is a waste of energy.

A day without problems is a day
without answers.

The 2% that someone is not should not outweigh the 98% that they are...

Stars are more visible during the night
but they were made to shine all the time.

The greatness of an action is not measured in what was done, but is recognized by how much it needed to be done.

Because you have more does not make you more, because you have less does not make you less; do what you can with what you have and your value will be immeasurable.

Do not underestimate your possibilities;
God has never had a perfect vessel to
flow through, He takes what is
available and uses it...

Just because the times are bad
doesn't mean that people have to
be bad. Use the good that is in you
to make times a little better.

It will get better for you.

Is it all good?

The support of good friends is
priceless, say thank you
for all they do.

Sometimes it is better to just let someone else do the work.

You are always appreciated by someone.

Be where you need to be is one way
to go where you want to be.

Help yourself so that helping others is natural.

Talk is cheap that's why it doesn't cost much to have a good conversation.

Running from problems only gets you to another problem faster.

Let the people that are good to you know how much you appreciate them; show the people that are bad to you how much you love them.

Today is a good day

Make amends not enemies.

I'm going to say it again, please and thank you is the meat and potatoes of courtesy.

This is a heads up. It is difficult to make
a good decision based upon bad advice.

Before this day is over think about
going to get some ice cream.

*No matter how great looking or fast
a car is it still has to stop
at a red light.*

Make sure it counts.

Not everything, just some of our tastes change.

*Appreciate those who wear the
uniform of service.*

I can't take the time because it is not mine to snatch, but I will take the time that is available to let go of and hold on to.

The road to happiness is better
traveled with companions.

The mirror will show you what you see but can never show you what you know; know that you are beautiful.

Marlon P. Weaver

Don't stop being you unless you
want to be you but better.

116

Smirk once in a while to see if
anyone else gets the joke.

We are not alone; everything is going to be alright.

Everyone wants to accept the credit but
no one wants to take the blame.

We will worry about tomorrow on tomorrow; right now it's still today.

There is still a lot to learn from puppy love.

You are worth receiving respect,
especially when you give it.

The difference between life and death is one breath. We only have one chance to improve the impression that's left. Our words and actions need to be our best.

Marlon P. Weaver

Let's go get it.

124

We smile everyday sometimes no thanks
to others, but they are welcome
to it anyway.

Make it special, do something unforgettable.

As time winds down for the day, let's not just settle for all that has transpired so far, but let's choose to consider how much of the day remains and make the absolute best of it.

One day I am going to be walking and probably bump into myself. My hope is that one of me, the better me has the courage to tell the other one he is going in the wrong direction.

Grab onto life and don't let go...
tickle it like crazy so the laughter
doesn't stop.

Wisdom is hindsight being responsibly applied to foresight.

When I was younger I didn't know how much I knew; Now that I'm older I know how much I didn't know.

The difference between education and learning is as listening to music and making it.

Sometimes it is better to turn the other cheek.

Marlon P. Weaver

I love my daughter.

Onward

About the Author

Marlon Weaver, a retired military veteran, credits his parents, the lessons that he learned growing up, and his experiences in the military to be the inspiration for his positive perspective which is recognized by his peers. He has published articles in the Bangor Daily News and has appeared in several television news broadcasts that highlight positive community connections. Marlon Weaver is a graduate of Penobscot Job Corps, Eastern Maine Community College, New England School of Broadcasting and Husson University where he is pursuing his MBA. Originally from Waterbury, Connecticut, he lives in Bangor, Maine, with his daughter and many good friends.

Made in the USA
Charleston, SC
03 June 2013